Giraffes

Kate Riggs

CREATIVE EDUCATION

seedlings

Published by Creative Education
P.O. Box 227, Mankato, Minnesota 56002
Creative Education is an imprint of
The Creative Company
www.thecreativecompany.us

Design and production by Ellen Huber
Art direction by Rita Marshall
Printed in the United States of America

Photographs by Bigstock (olaf herschbach, Musat, Naveen
Prabhu, Albert Trujillo), CanStock (Musat), Dreamstime
(Patricia Kullberg), Getty Images (Richard Du Toit, Art Wolfe),
iStockphoto (DenGuy, Dirk Freder, Hazlan Abdul Hakim,
Dieter Hawlan, irakite, Jandee Jones, Christian Musat),
Shutterstock (Jeff Grabert, Christian Musat), Veer (apgestoso)

Library of Congress Cataloging-in-Publication Data
Riggs, Kate.
Giraffes / by Kate Riggs.
p. cm. — (Seedlings)
Includes index.
Summary: A kindergarten-level introduction to giraffes,
covering their growth process, behaviors, the lands they call
home, and such defining physical features as their long necks.
ISBN 978-1-60818-276-3
1. Giraffe—Juvenile literature. I. Title.

QL737.U56R54 2012
599.638—dc23   2011044741

First Edition
9 8 7 6 5 4 3 2 1

TABLE OF CONTENTS

Hello,
giraffes!

Giraffes are tall animals. They live in Africa.

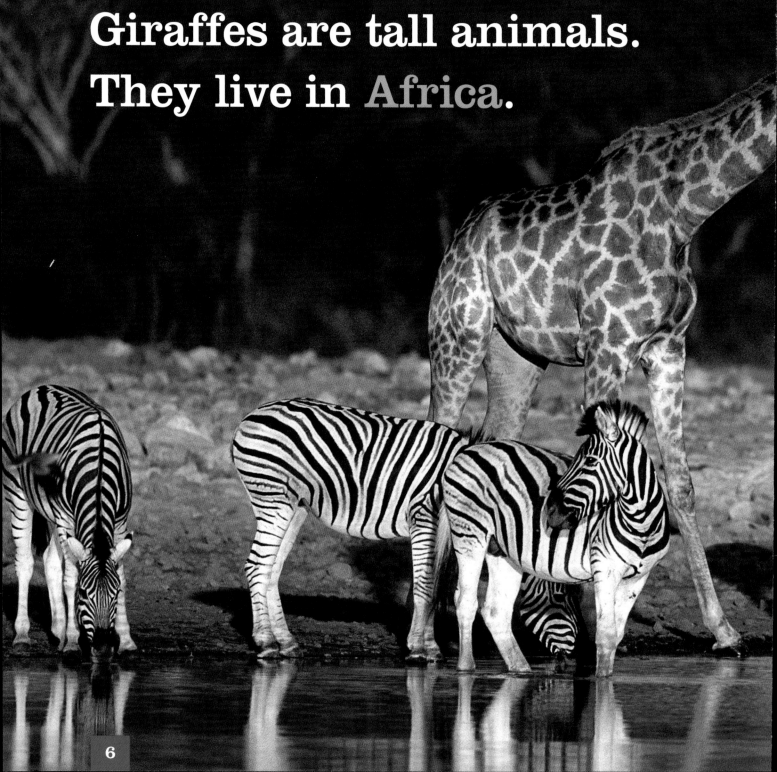

Giraffes have long necks.

They have
long legs,
too. Giraffes
can run fast.

Giraffe fur is yellow or white. It has brown spots. Giraffes have bumps on their heads called horns.

Giraffes eat plants.
They use their
long necks to reach
leaves on tall trees.

13

A baby giraffe is called a calf. A calf lives with other giraffes in a herd.

Giraffes can sleep standing up. They do not need much sleep. They spend most of the time eating.

Goodbye, giraffes!

Picture a Giraffe

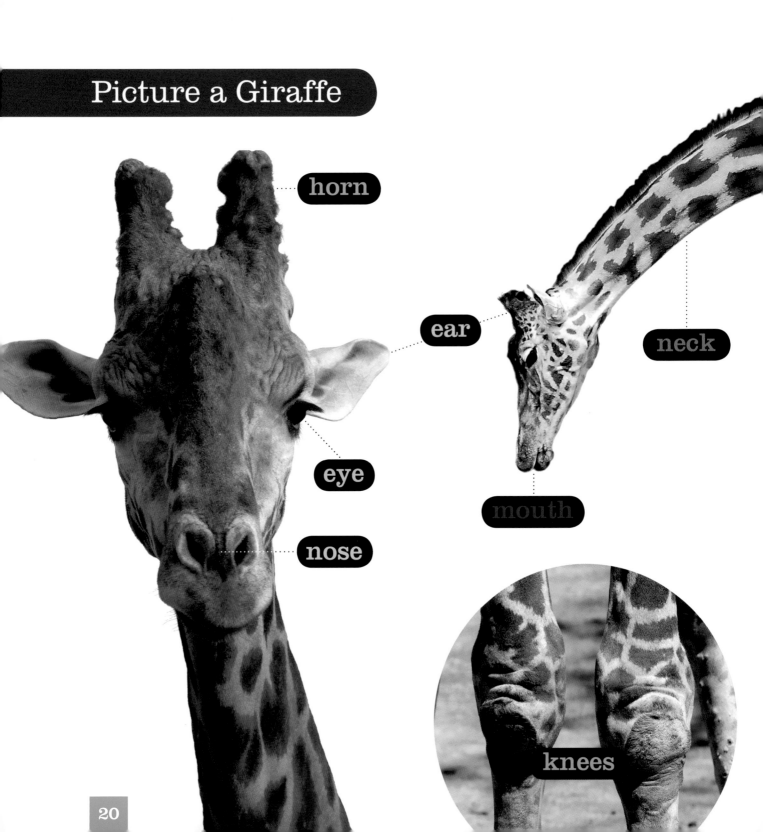

horn

ear

neck

eye

mouth

nose

knees

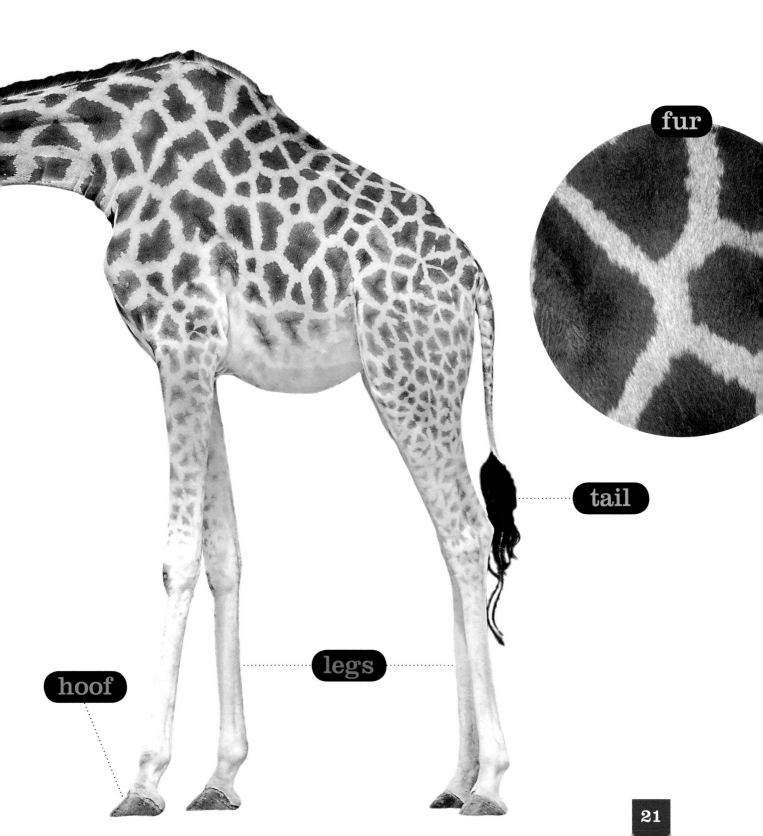

fur

tail

legs

hoof

Words to Know

Africa: the second-biggest piece of land in the world

fur: the short hair of an animal

herd: a large group of animals that live together

Read More

Galvin, Laura Gates. *New Baby Giraffe*.
Norwalk, Conn.: Soundprints, 2001.

Pingry, Patricia. *Baby Giraffe*.
Nashville: CandyCane Press, 2003.

Web Sites

DLTK's Jungle and Rainforest Animal Crafts: Giraffe Activities
http://www.dltk-kids.com/animals/jungle-giraffe.htm
Choose a craft to do. Have a grown-up help you.

Giraffe Online Jigsaw Puzzle
http://www.first-school.ws/puzzlesonline/animals/giraffe.htm
Pick the number of pieces. Put together a puzzle of a giraffe.

Index